WHY KISS A FROG?
YOUR PRINCE IS OUT THERE!

Every Woman's Complete Self-Help Guide to Friends, Lovers and The Search for Her Perfect Partner!

Men's honest answers to all women's questions, about men.

Finally find out what he's really thinking about…You!

MICHAEL McGAHEY

From The Creators Of WHY SLEEP ALONE? Vol. I. For Men!
©2002 BBE, Inc. McGahey / Newman

This book is a work of fiction. Places, events, and situations in this story are purely fictional. Any resemblance to actual persons, living or dead, is coincidental.

1stBooks - rev. 03/04/03

FIRST EDITION

WHY Kiss A FROG?
Your Prince Is Out There!

WHY KISS A FROG?
YOUR PRINCE <u>IS</u> OUT THERE!

This book is dedicated to Michelle.
The love of my life...my friend, my lover and my
perfect partner.
You will be my inspiration forever.

A true story…

Standing all alone one day not so long ago, I asked a question.
The kind of questions you ask yourself a thousand times a day, never really expecting any answers.

I asked, *"Will I be lonely forever?"*

Much to my surprise and even my fear…I received an answer.
To this day, I'm still not quite sure where it came from.

It was a voice in my head, but it sure wasn't me.

The voice said,

"Loneliness is like tomorrow.
It is going to come…and it is going to go."

Whoever you are, wherever you are, Thank you.
You were so right.

x

Contents

"*Very few have said so much by saying so little, so well.*"

www.readinghismind.com

Contents

WHY KISS A FROG?
YOUR PRINCE IS OUT THERE!

A Gift...

I have had many heroes in my life. As a result, I have had many teachers.

Truth be told, not all my teachers have been heroes, but all of my heroes have been amazing teachers. Most of them I will never meet and yet, I know them all as intimately as my oldest of friends.

I learned a valuable life-lesson long ago, (from one of my greatest heroes and certainly my greatest teacher) that you can learn something from virtually every person that you meet, and certainly every situation that you observe.

He said to me, "Learn from the good and discard the bad."

The lesson here is a simple one. You can learn just as much from someone else's mistakes, as from their successes. You can also learn as much from someone else's mistakes and successes, as your own. Sometimes, (if you're paying attention) even more.

He went on to teach me that, "there just aren't enough days in one's life-time to make all the mistakes or have all the successes yourself, so you must learn 'how to learn' from other people quickly, or you will waste your time and you will eventually waste your life."

It is a rare gift to learn how to learn.

As children, we are so innocently open to it.

We meet every new lesson with open arms and a smile.

When you think about it, we really have no choice.

What would have happened to you in your life if you had never learned how to walk, how to speak, or how to read?

It is a rare gift to learn how to learn.

Then if we are fortunate enough, the most wonderful of all gifts… is to learn how to pass it on.

For a fleeting moment in time, the student becomes the teacher.

It has been said many times that there is no new information, only new teachers and new students.

This I embrace and agree with whole-heartedly.

The messages here are simple and time tested. They will work, if you let them.

As you read and re-read this book…learn the gift.

If you should find any of the lessons here of value… give the gift – and pass them on.

Then, for that fleeting moment in time, the most wonderful of all gifts…*you* will become the teacher.

Who knows…maybe it's your turn to become someone's hero.

Inspired by the Lifetime of works created by: **Gilda Scofano.**

- CHAPTER 1-
Introduction and Inspirations

Welcome everyone to **WHY KISS A FROG?** Your Prince <u>IS</u> out there!

Here is a glimpse into the thoughts and minds of the strangest creatures that you'll ever encounter on this planet... **Men!**

A true story...

One night, a few years ago a very dear friend of mine and I were invited out to a dinner with a gorgeous woman – and *seven* of her female friends. It was their weekly 'girl's night out' and as luck would have it, she and her friends thought it might be fun to invite a couple of 'eligible' bachelors along. As dangerous and potentially volatile as this situation might seem, my friend and I were eager to accept. I had been trying for months to get a date with this woman and I wasn't going to miss my chance, any chance, at spending some time with her. After all, I was a single guy living and working in Miami Beach, and I had... "Everything to gain and nothing to lose!"

But I'll go over that again in a moment.

The evening started out normally enough with introductions and pleasantries being made all around. All of the women were in their late-twenties to early-thirties and ranged from 'average looking' to 'drop-dead gorgeous'. All of them were reasonably successful in their professional lives ranging in vocation from hair-stylist to police officer. One, the best looking and most intelligent of the bunch, was even studying to be a practicing psychologist!

The conversation was lively and the wine flowed freely. The women appeared ambivalent to the fact that we were men and almost immediately began to engage us in earnest discussions about the men in their lives. As the evening wore on and the conversation became more frank, it became obvious to both my friend and I that we were privy to something few men ever get to witness – women talking to other women about men!

The evening turned into a wonderful "question and answer" session. Honest questions by them, and truly honest answers by us, about why we men do the things we do.

Being men, we felt like we could speak as reasonable authorities on the subject!

We realized *two* things that evening that would ultimately change our lives forever. What became apparent to us right from the outset is that men are, for the most part, clueless when it comes to how to properly approach and introduce themselves to women. Over and over the women took turns relating to us stories of how a guy had approached her in public, only to make a complete jerk of himself. Men, it was determined, simply do not know how to properly address a woman – especially if he is nervous and looking to win a date for himself.

The next most obvious thing that came to light over the course of the evening is that women, on average, have no idea what or how men think in terms of these situations or relationships. Perhaps because they are the 'yin' to our 'yang', we discovered that women often misinterpret what we men are thinking and generally do a less than perfect job of assessing the entire 'male' approach to things.

The light went off in our heads almost immediately and before long my partner and I had written and successfully marketed an audio book on CD format for men entitled **"WHY SLEEP ALONE?"**

It was a journey to try to help men everywhere learn what was so obvious to us, and judging by the stories we were hearing from women, completely foreign to most of them.

Understand, here is my standard disclaimer – we don't claim to be geniuses, or a couple of Don Juan's, but what these women were asking us sure made us feel like we knew a whole lot more of something than their men did.

So with **WHY SLEEP ALONE? VOL.I**, we decided to address what we knew best. Teach men how to meet and treat women. And it worked! This was amazing to be a part of.

From the E-mails to the conversations to the interviews. Men were learning how to do what we had already learned to do, just by watching other men. We had watched the good ones *and* the bad ones. The winners and the losers. Learning what to do, and more importantly what not to do.

But then came the amazing part. We realized that still, the lion's share of the conversations we were having, <u>even</u> with **WHY SLEEP ALONE? VOL. I**. being targeted at men…were still with women! Women, out there searching for "their perfect partners." All of the conversations were basically the same. All women really want to do is find their "Prince Charming."

Hence, "**WHY KISS A FROG?** – Every Woman's Complete Guide to Friends, Lovers and the Search for Her Perfect Partner!"

This is what men are really thinking about: Love, lust, friends and lovers, romance, infidelity, insecurities... and what they are really thinking about *you* ladies.

You and your search for *your* perfect partner.

Questions that you wanted honest answers to.

Men's honest answers to your real-life questions.

This is our attempt to help women understand a little bit about how men approach love and relationships coupled with some very practical advice on how to find your 'perfect partner'. Living proof that people can (and do) grow and learn from their experiences provided there is a will to do so. I have *learned* how to make extraordinarily positive changes in my life, and now, armed with this information, so can you!

Loneliness is like tomorrow...
It is going to come, and it is going to go.

This book is therefore a testament to the fact that successful relationships have a lot more to do with learned behavior patterns than happenstance or just 'lightning striking'. There are rules to the road and all the signposts are there if you are willing to look for them and learn from them. Men are, after all, reasonably simple creatures once you understand the basics.

We are not all monsters nor are we completely bereft of feelings and emotions. Though sometimes we can be far less complex than women emotionally, we too have patterns and behaviors that you can learn to read and respond to easily and more effectively.

Sounds difficult huh? Well, I've got news for you…. it is.

They say, "The journey of a thousand miles in the wrong direction, doesn't get you any closer to where you really wanted to go." So we have to try to help you to understand your direction, and where you really want to go. And most importantly whom you want to go there with.

So sit back, relax and get comfortable.

Light a candle, run a bath and get ready to learn how to *not* SLEEP ALONE!

Not just for tonight…but for every night.

Your handsome prince *is* out there, but you are going to have to learn how to get out there and find him!

NOTE:

The following is a frank question and answer session. We offer this to you, the female reader, in an effort to further clarify the difference in the way men think compared to women.

All your questions will be preceded by a *Q:*

We compiled these questions and attempted to provide 'typical' male answers hoping that the information contained herein will assist you in achieving your goal of reading his mind and finding your prince.

Welcome ladies to **WHY KISS A FROG?**

- CHAPTER 2-
Everything to gain and nothing to lose!

This chapter is going to be the cornerstone of all we are going to discuss in this book. We will state this for you as simply and as clearly as we can:

By effectively meeting and interfacing with eligible single men you have…

"Everything to gain and nothing to lose!"

In short ladies, you can't win a prize if you don't first buy a ticket.

If an opportunity to meet a good man presents itself – for Heaven's sake take it!

Chance encounters, blind dates, seemingly boring and uninteresting dinner invitations have resulted in more successful introductions and long-lasting relationships than anyone can count. However, you must take that first crucial step. Get out there and make yourself available!

In life as in relationships:
You miss 100% of the shots you <u>don't</u> take!

You cannot find your prince while sitting at home and watching the Home Shopping Channel. We are not about to tell you ladies how to dress or even necessarily what to say, but we can tell you that if you do not get out there and put yourself in circulation (so to speak) your chances of finding Mr. Right are horribly slim. To find a good guy you must first see *and be seen*. It really is that simple!

Here is the basic mathematics of it. He's standing at the end of the bar…alone.

You're "the" woman at the other end of the bar…alone. He sees you, you see him.

Smiles are exchanged, and both your hearts start to beat a little bit faster.

We know that human nature takes over and makes *him* do the next natural thing…Nothing. RIGHT?

How many times in your life has this happened to you ladies?

It must be an awful lot, because it was one of the most frequently asked questions to us by all women.

Q: Why, if a man thinks you're attractive, does he wait for the woman to initiate the conversation?

The answer is actually quite simple. His fear of rejection. No one wants to get his or her feelings hurt. We had asked men to consider what was absolutely the worst thing that could have happened? You ladies <u>don't</u> like him. You say, "no", and he goes back to being alone. Ok…Next! BUT!!!!!! What if you, the interested woman at the other end of the bar, are just as afraid as he is and the conversation actually begins?

Congratulations! Now at least you're IN THE GAME! – both of you. Yes, you are probably going to have to kiss a few "frogs" in order to find your "prince", but remember to give it not only "A" shot, but give it your best shot.

You just never know.

Initiating conversations and making proper introductions is the first and most crucial step in any relationship. So why does it have to be so difficult?

Well, when you think of it – there are really only two basic motivators in life and everything in life can (and *does!*) relate to them. 'Pain vs. Pleasure'. The handsome man over at the end of the bar does not approach you because his fear of the pain (of rejection) outweighs his desire for pleasure. Fear of rejection happens to be one of the strongest of the human emotions. So, remember what we said about "Everything to gain and nothing to lose"? What would you risk to be just a little bit happier? Your already alone…you can't be any *more* alone, right?

Another way to state this is 'Fear vs. Desire'. You don't want to appear too eager to talk with him either, because your fear of appearing desperate out-paces your desire to get to know him. Hence, you fail to give off the right signals and he quickly loses interest and moves on. Congratulations! You BOTH blew it again!

The point is, most things in life – and in relationships – can be traced back to these two basic motivators. Interestingly enough, both are remedied by your willingness and ability to overcome your fear and your anxieties. Sure, there are lots of frogs out there, but there are a good number of terrific guys too! Your ability to conquer your inhibitions and let your need for pleasure overcome your fear of failure, can (and *will*!) pave the way for you to meet that someone special. You have – "Everything to gain and nothing to lose!"

It all starts with you! You can do it! Practice being more out-going. Put yourself in a position where you can meet other single people. Get out there and start having fun and, by all means, if an attractive man appears in your life, seize the opportunity to make the appropriate introductions and strike up a conversation.

Repeat after me – "Everything to gain and nothing to lose!" There! Good!

Now again and again, over and over, until you really *believe* it.

Remember that one of my favorite sayings is "Winners never quit and quitters never win!"

> ***Life is all about taking chances
> and seizing opportunities
> when and where they present themselves.***

Men have traditionally accepted their role as the aggressors in a relationship. A role, quite frankly, we often can do without!

Things *are* changing however. Nowadays it is not completely unheard of for a woman to make the initial introduction to the man. In fact, it's becoming increasingly more in vogue for women to take charge of their destiny and actively pursue men. There is no reason why a woman cannot stroll up and start a conversation with a man, provided it is done in a tasteful and straightforward matter.

There is no reward without risk. Believe me.

Happiness and a healthy relationship are worth the risk of a few bad conversations.

A few "Frogs." So, have the conversations and take the risks.

You'll be happy that you did.

Q: So, where does a nice girl go to find men on this planet?

Well, anywhere really. There are guys all over, in bars for sure, but also in some of the less obvious places. For instance, you might consider enrolling in a night course at your local community college, or maybe joining a local charity group.

There are always special travel packages available for singles, tropical resorts, cruise ships. Alternatively, there are numerous dating services, ski lodges, museums, and art galleries all teeming with available men of every size and description. Heck – there are even available men right in your own neighborhood food store.

The trick is to get out there and be active. By meeting new people and going new places, you increase your chances of meeting someone special exponentially. "Everything to gain and nothing to lose." If you fail to take the initiative to get out there and 'rub elbows' you condemn yourself to a lifetime of boredom and old TV re-runs...alone.

So be bold and get active! Practice engaging men in conversation. Why not strike up a conversation with the guy next to you on the bus or at the record store? Or the cute guy who works at the gym you frequent? Who knows? That perfect stranger could turn out to be the one person in this world that is just perfect for you!

Before long – you'll be on your way to finding your very own prince charming.

It *will* happen, because you are going to *make it* happen!

- CHAPTER -3-
Love Potions And Flirting

This is all about how to get a *good* guy.

Q: Are you, a man, going to teach women how to flirt with men?

In a word…yes!

Ladies, this is the real truth and nothing but the truth. Honest answers, that's what you wanted, and that's what you're going to get! At least from our perspectives.

I have a strong feeling that you'll find this *pretty* accurate, and without question an eye opener. Maybe even a jaw dropper? We're definitely going to break a couple of your life long "male" conceptions, or misconceptions, here.

To begin with, whether women want to believe it or not, in the world of men and women, the females clearly hold most of the power. Men are programmed to chase the girls, and the girls are trained to thwart the advances of men. In short – "we want what you ladies have got." Simple. The only problem is that the definition of 'it' varies depending upon which sex you are talking to.

So first, we have to re-establish some basic ground rules that women seem to forget from time to time…**MEN <u>ARE</u> EASY!**

Q: Do you really think women don't know that?

I have heard over and over in conversations with single women that, "I really like this guy but he just doesn't respond." Subsequently, I've had hundreds conversations with men about this same subject and they all, without exception, say the same thing…

Women just don't understand us! Don't they know just how "easy" we really are?

We men lust after you women, and you women do the choosing and decide which men can gain access. And that's OK. We're not complaining…really.

So, the question remains; can we men teach you women how to flirt with us and therefore make it easier for both of us to get what we ultimately want?

All right then, let's not get ahead of ourselves here. Let's instead assume that at least initially, a woman will flirt with a man to gain his attention and perhaps even prompt him into summoning up the courage to make an introduction. What then should a girl do? What are the gestures that a woman should use to entice the male of the species?

The art of flirting with males is relatively straightforward and one in which women really *do* hold most of the cards. As guys, our 'mojo' is almost constantly at work. When confronted with members of the opposite sex, we routinely send out enough 'signals' to fill an air traffic controller's screen. Women for their part need only to reciprocate to the 'tone' we are beaming their way. What you choose to pursue after that is your own business!

But how to get our attention? – Let's start with the basics.

Flirting Rule #1: *Men are attracted to women who look good*

Jeez…No secret here! It's true that men are principally motivated by what they see. That is to say that we men are at least initially attracted to members of the opposite sex who look good to us. This does not necessarily mean the best looking women, but rather the women who make an effort to enhance their most obvious assets.

It has been said many times that, "Men fall in love with their 'eyes' and women fall in love with their ears."

While women will listen closely to what a man *says*, men are almost exclusively attuned initially to how a woman *looks*. Beautiful hair, straight teeth, well groomed hands and nails – these are all things that guys look for and find themselves attracted to in a woman. She could speak Latin for all we care, but if she looks good then – wham! – our rockets will kick us into high gear.

As simple as it sounds, a great place to start flirting is with the good old "hair fix" or the "hair flip" as some call it.

This is *the* great opening signal. It's called 'preening', and it works on us every time. It works in a car, in the bookstore, in a club – everywhere. It sends the signal to the guy that you want to look nice *for him*.

Ego – remember ladies, we're dealing with a man's ego. "Look nice for him."

So go ahead and flip that long beautiful head of hair of yours. You will get our attention!

Flirting Rule #2: *Smile*

There is an old saying in the southern United States that says, "Girls love a man with a plan, and boys love a girl with a smile." A great smile is always inviting to the male – particularly if it is directed at us! As simple as this sounds as well, we men want to believe that out of everyone in the room, you are smiling at us.

Men will actually argue with each other, "She smiled at me!"

"What are you blind? She smiled at me!"

This happens to us all the time. As a point of reference, men are territorial by nature. So if you smile at him, he'll always look to defend his territory. You!

Which leads us to…

Flirting Rule #3: *Make direct eye contact*

Super important! Without making positive and direct eye contact a guy cannot be sure that a girl is interested in him or just adjusting her contact lenses. Combine direct eye contact with your best smile, and he'll get the hint!

Flirting Rule #4: *Men do need a little bit of a chase*

You are going to have to make him work for it a little bit. This is unfortunate, but true. Why do there have to be games? Personally – I hate games, but I hate taxes too, and they are both unfortunately just a part of life. The male ego is a funny and extremely fragile thing. Think of the man you want as a fisherman in a small boat. Fishermen want to catch the fish, they are out there to catch the fish, but there is no sport in the darn thing jumping into the boat by itself!

He wants and needs to feel like he "caught" it. That's just the male ego at work. Let him "work the line" a little. He'll feel better about himself if he does.

IMPORTANT NOTE: <u>Do not</u> sleep with a man that you are looking for a serious relationship with on the first date! Ladies, do not sleep with him! Period. Yes, he wants you to sleep with him, because he's a guy and that's just what we do, but not on the first date! No matter how great the attraction! *He* wants *you* to want him, but deep inside, he wants you to be the kind of girl he can trust. This is crucial. He needs that psychologically more than he needs the physical contact.

Ladies, you *never* get a second chance to make a first impression. <u>Never!</u>

He has a *secret* agenda, and we'll get to that deeper in the next chapter, but believe me…

he *needs* to trust you. We'll tell you why that's so important in a minute.

And finally…

Flirting Rule #5: *Play to his ego*

We admit that on some basic fundamental level we men are all shallow, a little self-centered and largely ego-driven. Hey, we're guys, OK? So go ahead and compliment us on our muscles, or our cars, or our clothing. Please laugh at our jokes, even if they are terrible, and try to take a genuine interest in what we have to say. In a word be "nice".

Almost any woman can have any guy she wants, at least initially, by demonstrating even a mild interest in things that are dear to him.

Q: Should the women initiate?

Q: Should they buy a man a drink, or should they offer a man they are attracted to their phone number, even if he hasn't asked for it?

Q: Does this make them look desperate or too forward, or does it just make them look cheap?

Great questions? Same answer over and over again.

She has, "Everything to gain and nothing to lose!"

He may really want to talk to you, but may be ultimately intimidated by you. We hear all the time about the most Beautiful Women in the World who are the loneliest because men are just too afraid to approach them. So the answer is yes, absolutely initiate. I have a very dear friend in a wonderful marriage, and his wife asked him to marry her!

Never forget that the male will principally be flirting with you with just one thing in mind, and it initially has very little to do with reading poetry by candlelight or debating religious or social beliefs! So long as you understand and acknowledge the rules of the road, you can safely navigate the sensuous world of flirting with men without coming off as 'cheap' or 'tawdry' – though secretly, sometimes depending on the man, that would be all right too!

Smile! Be open, complimentary and even touchy. But always remember, that deep down inside that he wants you to be a "good girl" so he can trust you in the future. He wants you in the boat, but *he* wants to pull you there.

If you speak to men in healthy relationships, all of their stories of true love start with, "I saw her, and I knew instantly that she was the one, and she never made it easy on me in the beginning!"

Q: *So, are you suggesting that women play hard to get?*

I'm not suggesting you *play* hard to get at all. Be a little hard to get, just for your own self-esteem and self-respect. One of the greatest turn offs in men and women is desperation. We all know this person, or have maybe even been this person at some time in our lives, and it isn't pretty. Fight at all costs, the looks, the sounds, or even the smells that come along with the horrible emotion that is desperation.

If it's meant to be, it can wait a day or two, and it will probably be a whole lot better and a whole lot more intense if it does. Just try it and you'll see that we're right.

If he is your Mr. Right, if he is your prince – then take your time! Forever starts today, and that's a long, long time.

- CHAPTER 4-
<u>The Sins Of Another Man</u>

For some strange reason women, more than men, seem to be haunted by past love affairs. Generally speaking, women appear to be more affected by their past relationships than do men. Now granted, this is a tremendous generalization, and we do want to make it clear that we *are* painting with broad strokes here! However, it is probably fair to say that men are somewhat more compartmentalized, and do not seem so much in the habit of comparing new partners to old, except when it comes to sex for some reason, but we'll address that again in a short moment.

Take for example this very common female statement, "I'm never going to fall in love again. I'm just so tired of being hurt!" I feel that this has got to be one of the most ridiculous statements any human being can make.

First of all, the very next person you meet after a sour love affair has got to start with a clean slate. Nothing else would be fair to him – or to you! If you have had a string of unsuccessful relationships, or have suffered from men who have treated you badly, maybe even have been unfaithful to you in the past – then one of two things is happening. Either 'A': your shopping in the wrong 'store' and need to reappraise the kind and type of men you date. Or, 'B': you're making the same kind of mistakes over and over again.

You keep changing the players, but the final score of the game is always the same.

Him 1 to You Zero. Another broken heart.

It's not them.

Contrary to popular female belief, men are not all pond scum. By allowing past history to cloud your thinking you just might ruin any chance of something wonderful happening to you in the future. What if the very next fella turned out to be your dashing prince, only you are still hurting from a past relationship and are too pre-occupied to give this man a fair shake? You're about to ruin any chance at something wonderful, because you're still stinging from the last momentary relationship setback. And that's how you have to look at this – as a "momentary setback", not the end of your life.

Jettison the baggage and remain forward in your thinking. The sins of one man must not be allowed to taint all future relationships.

By letting go of the past and getting rid of all the garbage associated with a failed relationship you not only lighten your own emotional burden, but also set yourself up for more pleasure down the road. Whatever lousy thing a guy has done or said, you must resist the temptation to carry this emotional baggage over into your next relationship.

Not all men are created equal. 'Some guys', we will concede – are just plain *idiots*. Nevertheless, a truly smart girl should know enough to separate the good apples from the bad and move on in her own life. Let's explore this in a little more detail.

If one guy you dated was a lousy lover, would you assume that all men were lousy lovers? If the next guy you dated by chance was also a lousy lover, does that confirm that all men are lousy lovers? Obviously not!

All men and all women are separate and individual entities unto themselves, and must be treated that way. You cannot judge – ever. If you judge you will end up in a place you don't want to be! I promise you. He may look like the last guy, even act a 'little' like the last guy, but that is to be expected. It's called personal taste. Yours! But this is where it should end. He is not the other guy.

So do yourself a favor ladies, treat each man separately and avoid becoming that most loathsome of all female creatures – 'the man hater'. Whatever demons you may harbor, whatever dragons you may have faced and whatever luggage you may have stored in that mental/sexual closet of yours – lose them! Otherwise you may risk sabotaging a perfectly good relationship based on what has transpired in a previous one.

> *Most people would rather be 'comfortably unhappy' than 'uncomfortably happy!'*

I would like to tell you about the love of my life because the story is so great, and it deserves to be heard. When I met her, she had already been married. Unhappily, thank goodness for me.

If she had been "that" type of person, the "I'm never going to let another man into my heart because they're all pond scum" person, then we never would have had even a chance at the amazing life that we've created for ourselves.

The real problem here is the possibility for what is called a "Self-Fulfilling Prophecy." *You* expect the man to treat you poorly. You expect the relationship to go badly because they *all* have in the past. At the first bump in the road, you will unknowingly destroy the relationship because you feel like it's coming anyway, and that's what you feel you deserve. You figure you may as well just get it over with. You think subconsciously that the relationship is truly doomed, so you quietly destroy it from the inside out. You create the outcome without ever knowing that you did it to yourself or to your potential prince. Then you just go back to being unhappy, where you were more comfortable. Unhappy and alone. People rarely realize that they are doing this kind of personal "sabotage."

They would rather be "comfortably unhappy" than "uncomfortably happy."

You have to remember that not only do you deserve this chance at happiness, but so does he! He's a "new" player, not the same old heartbreaker you're used to. So give him a chance. Let him make a couple of his own mistakes.

Then learn to ask yourself this question, "Am I happy?" If not, you risk transposing this unhappiness into your next relationship. Every opportunity for love deserves a fresh start. A blank canvass upon which you and your partner can create what is uniquely yours without being burdened by the sins of the past. You owe this to yourself!

Ok, let's now go back and address the statement we made about men and the comparisons they make with their past sexual partners. The only place where men tend to hold on to the past is honestly…*sex.*

We have had several male friends along the way who have told us that they really loved the woman that they were with in a relationship today, but that a past lover was really the one who had rocked their boat when it came to the bedroom. Shame on them. Making love ladies, <u>and</u> gentlemen if you're listening, is all about communication. Just like all relationships and all facets of relationships, you have to talk.

Women are not mind readers. People are not mind readers. Tell your partner what you want. A lot of times I have had women tell me that they've always wanted to do things "like that", in the bedroom but they were too afraid to initiate the conversations.

Remember ladies, communication is a two way street.

Ask him what he likes. And don't be too embarrassed to tell him what you like too.

Try some new things! No, it doesn't make you look cheap or easy. You may even surprise yourself and find a new fire where some old flames were flickering.

Just don't hold it against him where he may have learned those things.

The past is the past…leave it there.

- CHAPTER 5-
R.E.S.P.E.C.T. Yourself!

This is a subject that we want to focus on carefully, because quite frankly this is where we feel most women fail when it comes to relationships. So-called 'hard luck' women are almost a proverb in this world and largely the result of women who are not able or willing to respect themselves enough to *demand* that they be treated better by the men they choose to meet and enter a relationship with.

Next to "Everything to gain and nothing to lose," this may be the most important concept in the entire book. As a matter of fact, it may even be more important. Even if you get up the nerve to speak to the man of your dreams or even just let him speak to you, then the relationship is doomed to failure without this crucial element. Because deep down inside, you don't *feel* like you're worthy of the relationship at all.

How many times have you heard a woman lament about being 'hard done by' her man? It is the very stuff old-country-love songs are made of! Alcoholics, drug abusers, compulsive gamblers, men with tempers, men who steal, men who cheat, men who assault their women – they are all out there and some girls seem attracted to them like moths to light. The truth is; most of these women allow themselves to be victimized over and over again by habitually making the wrong choices when it comes to the type of men they choose to associate with.

Please do not misunderstand. *Anybody* can fall prey to the moral ambiguity and cruelty of an abusive male. There is no fault in this and such behavior is inexcusable and dead wrong on the part of the offending male! Rather the point is, there are a significant number of women who seem to repeat this cycle time and time again, with more-or-less the same kind of guy.

Boil away all the other contributing factors – social, economic and cultural – and what you are left with is a basic issue of self-respect. In this world ladies, rightly or wrongly – and like it or not, you are basically treated the way you allow yourself to be treated.

> *If you have no respect for yourself...then why should anybody else have any respect for you?*

Let me share with you a personal story as told from a man's perspective. Before I met the love of my life I was a thirty-something male, single, reasonably good-looking and earning a decent living. I had a great little place on the ocean, a sharp looking convertible, a bit of spending money and lets just say a couple of friends that weren't men. Unfortunately, I was still completely miserable.

I had spent years combing the bars searching for that one 'perfect partner' that I could share my life with. Instead, all I found was a seemingly endless succession of barflies and wanna-be models, most of them suffering from serious emotional issues, and in many instances, severe substance abuse problems.

So why was I having so much trouble finding my perfect partner?

Was it me, or was it all of them?

The real answer is…both.

First, for most men, even though it's difficult to get them to admit it in front of other men, most men are not that different from women when it comes to the 'concept' of a perfect partner. Forget the bravado. Forget the macho nonsense. Most men really just want one woman, the right woman. The one woman that ends what seems like the never ending blur of one-night-stands and empty physical relationships.

It's true ladies, and that's the hope. That's the silent ultimate goal.

Just one woman – the right woman.

Remember what we said in Chapter 3 about a secret agenda – well here's the secret. Whether he even knows it or not, every guy is quietly, secretly looking for the one woman that is "good enough to raise his children." She ultimately may or may not have been his best lover, she may or may not even be the best looking, but she's the one that isn't affected. She isn't ego based, she's reality based. That's the woman he wants to raise his children. The truth is, that kind of woman doesn't exist unless she respects herself first. If you have no respect for yourself…then why should anybody else have any respect for you?

Look, the lesson here is a simple one; you can spend your whole life caught in an endless cycle of losers, repeating the same kind of mistakes over and over again when it comes to members of the opposite sex.

Or, you can give some honest thought to **changing the way you think about yourself.**

Before you can meet anybody worth spending a lifetime with you have to first feel that you are worthy and deserving on the inside. You have to believe that you are not 'broken' emotionally or spiritually. It's all about self-love and a sense that you respect who and what you are, and that you demand that same respect from others.

Finding true love is directly related to self-love.
Develop one and you find the other.

The second reason that I couldn't find my perfect partner wasn't anyone else's fault except my own. I came to realize that "I" wasn't healthy in my own mind.

Here's what happened to me.

The long distance telephone call came late one night from a dear childhood friend of mine. He had moved to the West Coast and had created a wonderful healthy life for himself, complete with dream job, gorgeous wife and beautiful baby. The perfect life. I've always looked up to him and quietly envied his situation. To him it all seemed so clear.

What was his secret? What did he know that I, and so many of *us* were missing?

He said to me, "You deserve it. You deserve to be happy!"

I thought for a moment and said, "Of course I do."

He said, "No… you're saying the words, but you don't really believe the words yourself.

You really <u>are</u> worth it and you really <u>do</u> deserve *it*. You deserve to be happy!"

You have to respect yourself first, before you can really give yourself away to someone else, anyone else! These are only words until you give them meaning.

And the meaning is believing in *you!* You <u>are</u> worth it. You <u>do</u> deserve it.

For me it was a light! A bolt of lightning that lifted thirty some odd years of confusion and loneliness in an instant. "He's right! I am worth it. I do deserve it!"

People would tell me that I was really a good guy, but inside I wouldn't really believe them. People would even tell me that they loved me, and I wouldn't really believe them. Down deep inside, the only place where it really counted, I didn't respect myself. I didn't think I deserved to be happy. I didn't believe that I was worth it. And I didn't believe that I was worth being loved. And in an instant, it all changed. I had learned to control my thoughts. My thoughts then controlled my emotions and I was ready to let someone special in.

That's why this is so important and why I keep repeating it, because respecting yourself becomes the building blocks for all healthy relationships. Not <u>all</u> relationships, but all healthy relationships! This is where you have to honest with yourself.

Not all your relationships are healthy. But that's the key – healthy.

You can't expect to have a healthy relationship if you are not mentally healthy. And I wasn't. But the good news is – relax! It's easier to get there than you think. All it took for me was that one telephone call and a simple change in my perspective.

It's a choice. And now it's your turn. Here's how to do it…

Are you ready?

It is a choice!

You control your thoughts, and you can change your thinking in an instant. You control your thoughts and your thoughts control your emotions.

So, contrary to what you've been believing so far, by controlling your thoughts, you will control your emotions.

How many times have you heard someone say, "I'm so blue today, and I just can't snap out of it!" That's nonsense. You control your thoughts. You're not a mindless Zombie!

You deserve to be happy. You are worthy. You have to learn to respect yourself first before you can ever really give yourself away to someone else. All of this starts with *you*! Remember; you control your thoughts, your thoughts control your emotions and define your needs. Not the other way around. Your emotions do not control you or your thoughts... *you do.*

So ladies, here is your 'new' mental exercise because now, it's your turn to get healthy.

You work out your bodies for hours and hours a day, so now it's time to work out your minds. You'll have to say it, over and over, and believe it, for this to really make the difference.

You are worth it. You do deserve to be happy. Everyone does.

Not just the beautiful people. Not just the popular people. Not just the skinny people. Not just the rich people. Not just the people on TV... everybody!

I can give you the tools ladies, but you have to put them in motion for any of this to work for you. So believe it. Don't just say it to try to convince yourself.

Re-program yourself!

Re-program your subconscious self!

Everyone is different, and the difference is what makes you special. Say it over and over again and wait for the lightning to strike, because once you really believe it everything will change – for the better. From this day forward take control of your thoughts and demand more out of your life and the men you choose to date. You need and deserve to be respected. You will soon find that men will come to treat you the way you yourself expect to be treated.

So, by-pass the frogs and keep on the lookout for your handsome prince. It's all about R.E.S.P.E.C.T. Respect for yourself, and the respect you demand from the men in your life!

-CHAPTER -6-
The Bargain Bin

Ladies, it's time to talk honestly about "Bad Boys".

Some of you women are going to be **very** uncomfortable right now, because you know that we're talking about you. You love the rebel, or at least you think you do.

This is the guy that everyone else knows is so bad for you, but you can't seem to get enough of him.

He's probably really good looking…

And knows it.

He's probably really popular…

And knows it.

You're probably the envy of all your girlfriends…

And love it!

And you're probably secretly dying inside and just want to go somewhere where no one will hear you screaming from frustration.

Or, more accurately, just go somewhere where you can have another very lonely cry, by yourself.

He's a 'bad boy' all right. That popular icon of modern American culture – the strange and troubled one with careless hair and intense eyes, full, passionate and sensitive – but way too cool to care about anything in particular. Even you!

He's the one who doesn't call you for three days…on a weekend!

He's the one who makes plans with you for nine o'clock and cancels them at 11:45, after you've been sitting by the phone waiting and pacing.

Or the most frustrating… he's the one who, the only time you hear from him is 2:30 in the morning when you know in your heart that you weren't his first choice, but you allow yourself to be content with being on his list at all.

You know that you've all done this.

How do I know?

Because I'm not so proud to say that we've done it to you. All of it.

Q: So why do girls love this kind of guy?

Q: Why would an otherwise intelligent, modern woman subject herself to this kind of treatment?

There are several reasons actually.

Number one is what we just covered in RESPECT yourself.

Deep down inside, you think that this is all that you deserve.

That's just plain wrong!

You do deserve better – you are worth better!

The second reason some of us shop in the "Bargain Bin" is selfish in a backward way. I'll explain. There are people who subconsciously want to be the one that always helps the "lost puppy". The underdog. The wandering soul in the night and a hundred other romantic fantasies that all equate to the same misguided notion.

Somewhere close to their core, most women harbor a strong 'Mother Theresa' complex. A female's need to nurture can lead her to become involved with men that are woefully wrong for her, even harmful. The truth is most women can't help themselves – it's hardwired right into their collective conscious. She can fix him, mend what's broken inside and make him whole again.

> *Women are attracted to men believing they can change them, whereas men are attracted to women believing that they will never change.*

A woman feels she can 'change him', make him give up his evil ways and reform to a monogamous law-abiding lifestyle, free of late nights, loud motorcycles and whatever other vices he may have earned along his travels.

She dreams of a different life for the two of them. A world full of quaint bungalows where mini-vans line the streets and happy children play in sunbathed yards.

With her once infamous rebel at her side, she dreams of settling down to raise their children and experience the kind of wedded bliss featured in automobile advertisements and subdivision billboards.

Sound fantastic? Maybe. The plain truth is most women at some point in their single lives suffer from this illusion. The idea that they can transform an otherwise emotionally irresponsible lout into a mature and responsible father and provider.

As men, we are here to tell you gals that it simply does not work!

The trick, ladies, is to recognize these individuals for what they are – largely dysfunctional. These so-called 'misguided angels' represent a myth that is just that – a myth. Date them if you will, let them pluck out late-night ballads to you on their guitars, but do not, repeat DO NOT, think that you can change them. You cannot.

The element of danger and mystery should be present in every passionate relationship, but not dominate it.

A thinking woman who respects herself, and demands a certain level of respect in return from the men she meets and dates, must make an honest effort not to be fooled by or become addicted to the 'bad boy' types. If a good man likes and is attracted to you, then he will give you more than a pager number by which to reach him. He will return your calls within a reasonable period of time, and he will not leave you sitting by the phone crying your eyes out.

There is a third reason. There is also the element of human nature that makes us want what we can't have.

To control what we can't control. It's a classic situation that too many people fall into when it comes to their relationships with each other.

She thinks, *"If I could somehow help him, like the little lost puppy that he is."*

But what's really going on is; if she could somehow help him, then **she subconsciously feels a little better about herself.**

When you lack self-confidence inside, then helping others will subconsciously validate *you.* In reality this is only a quick fix, because it rarely, if ever, works. People may genuinely help the "lost puppies", if only for a moment or two, but because ultimately when the little "lost puppy" gets lost again, you're no better off than you were before you found them. And neither are they for the most part.

Sorry—I know it hurts, but it's true.

So remember, the next time you're shopping at the bargain store, you're just setting yourself up for a disappointment and you deserve better.

The choice is yours ladies. Bad boys have a time and a place. A little voyeurism in a gal's life is not such a bad thing. But, and herein lies our advice to you; do not expect to build a life or find true and lasting love with somebody that cannot remember your last name or lives in the back of a pick-up truck!

You may try to save him, but ultimately you probably are not going to really help him, and you sure aren't going to help yourself.

So do yourself a favor when it comes to 'bad boys'…and make the right choice!

That "bad boy' is really just a frog. You're still looking for your prince.

-CHAPTER 7-

<u>Why Kiss A Frog? Your prince IS out there!</u>

I was given a book years ago that was all about surrendering to the notion that no man is perfect. Women should just relax and stop putting so much pressure on themselves and just grab a man. Any man! Men are not perfect and you just have to deal with their imperfections.

(Sarcastically) Yes ladies, it's true – we're all losers, and all you women are just going to have to forgive us for being losers. We're so sorry.

Yeah right!

It sounds like this may have been written by someone who lacked a little R.E.S.P.E.C.T for herself and, no ladies, we men are not all losers!

I recently read a similar article on the Internet, and again it infuriated me. I think there is a responsibility that comes along with giving out emotional advice, and although I'm sure the people who wrote these books and articles meant well, my personal view is that "settling" for someone who isn't perfect "for you" is the worst advice you can give to anyone, anywhere.

Men or women!

The key here is not perfect, but "perfect for you." I think we have to begin here with a basic understanding.

All women are different, therefore, theoretically, all men should be different too…correct?

Is he a frog or is he a prince? Is he a dud or is he a stud? Ah, there is the question! By rough count, there are approximately 6 billion people in the world, and half of them are men.

So with 3 billion men on the planet, you would think that it would have to take a pretty strong pessimist to tell anyone to "settle" with anything less than someone perfect for them, with all of those people to choose from.

Seriously though, there are plenty of single men out there. The trick is finding the one guy who is right for you. In order to do this you're going to have to do a little culling. Assuming you know the type of man you are looking for. You are going to have to sort your way through a few frogs before you can find your prince.

The key is not finding the 'perfect man' but rather the man who is 'perfect for you'!

There are a couple of things to keep in mind when undergoing this process.

The first thing you are going to have to come to grips with is the idea of the 'perfect man'. This would be the guy who best fulfills all those qualities you judge to be most important in a man. Sort of your own 'personal little prince'!

I believe you should have a list of the things that you want in a man. You have a list for groceries for goodness sake. I think finding the love of your life is a little more important than what is for dinner! Would you agree? I thought so.

I had a list.

I had a very specific list. And to my amazement, the love of my life was "all that" and a whole lot more. But without the list, how would I have known what I was looking for – or not looking for. It was a simple list and may even sound obvious but you'd be surprised how many women I have met that had some of the bases covered, but just not all.

She had all of them and then some!

My "perfect woman" had to be: smart, beautiful, athletic, artistic, she had to be kind, and good with children, oh and she had to laugh at my jokes. (That was a tough one to find— trust me.) I wasn't looking for someone to take care of, or someone to take care of me. I was looking for a partner. But most importantly, the one quality that I had never found in any woman until I met her was that they had never seemed to bring out the best in *me*.

You are going to fall in love, *real love*, with the person that makes *you* feel the best about *yourself*. Period.

The next thing you are going to have to consider is that your quest to find a prince will involve a significant investment. The two principal things you are going to have to invest in order to find that perfect guy are: time and emotional energy.

It takes time to meet, date and get to know somebody. Contrary to popular belief, love, or at least the true and lasting kind, does not happen overnight!

First, you're going to have to invest some time in the relationship and really get to know the other person before you can make a reliable judgment as to whether or not he is a frog or a charming prince in disguise. Love at first sight does work sometimes in real life as well as in the movies, but sometimes even the most happily married couples grew to love each other over a reasonable period of time. It's the old notion of 'courting', and it's fun. Try it!

Second, there is a certain amount of emotional energy that must be invested in order to satisfy yourself that you are giving 100% to the relationship. Half-hearted efforts typically produce half-baked results. Every swing of the bat deserves all the emotional and intellectual focus you can bring to bear. The stakes are high and are nothing less than your spiritual and emotional happiness for the rest of your life. So do yourself a favor and satisfy yourself that – when it comes to a relationship – you gave it all that you've got. You'll be glad you did!

Bear in mind ladies that your journey from the desert to the well can, in fact, be a long one. And though you might not want to kiss all the frogs along the way, you are certainly going to have to sort through at least *a few* frogs to find your prince.

Some things worth having just take more time than others. Most new investments, just like most relationships, fail to produce substantial profits in the very short term. So don't get caught up looking for the short-term gain; try to be a 'long-term' player. Know what type of man you are looking for and *learn to invest your time and emotional energy accordingly.* There *is* one perfect man for you out there, somewhere…but you're going to have to find him.

Q: The statements that "All the good one's are taken!" Or, "All the great ones are married." Are they true?

That's just ridiculous. Your Prince is out there. Believe it! There *is* someone out there for everyone, without settling. Just make your own wish list and try to stick to it. You'll soon see who's the frog and who's the "Prince." Who is the dud and who is the "Stud"?

My only advice to all women is to make sure that he's a gentleman. He has to have honesty, integrity, manners, and 'looks' are only really important for the short term and are up to your own personal tastes. Try not to base your entire wish list on looks or you're in for a disappointment. That never works.

He should be romantic and generous, tender when he needs to be and passionate about you and your life. Stay away from manipulators if you can. These guys usually end up being a "dud". If you are constantly second guessing him and/or yourself, then you're going to run out of energy for the really important issues of the romance.

Just make sure he's the person that makes you feel the best about yourself.

Q: A lot of single and divorced women are trying the Internet dating services.
Q: What do men think about Internet dating?

I think it's great. What better way is there to see a lot of potential guys without having to sit on a bar stool all night. All of the "wish list" is right there in front of you, written out by him, and most of them even have a picture for you to see if that part of the "list" is super important to you.

Note: Watch out for the picture that was taken 10 years ago!

I guess you're still eventually going to have to go out on a date, but I think a lot of the preliminary, uncomfortable moments can be eliminated.

Remember ladies that relationships really are like investments. They are investments in your time, your bodies, your emotions and your hearts.

You are going to fall in love, real love, with the person that makes you feel the best about yourself. Period. That's the man who will be your prince. Forever.

He is *your* guy and he treats you well and loves you even when you are being silly. That's the best.

-CHAPTER 8-
The Hunting Trip

I read an article on the Internet recently that was telling women, "How to date like a man". The article had a very negative slant to it, and I must admit that I was a little confused by it. I understood why I was confused when I realized that the article was written by a woman.

Perhaps the confusion was due to how women lack the male's instinctive predatory nature. Or perhaps it is because women, unlike men, do not approach meeting and dating people in a logical, almost workman-like, fashion. Either way, I believe that women can learn a thing or two from men when it comes to dating. Let me explain…

The "Hunting" analogy in the title is the analogy that suits what "single men" do most accurately, but we've found that this particular concept makes most women extremely uncomfortable.

I'm not here to make anyone uncomfortable but, I believe that some of the more aggressive dating techniques, the basic concepts that men use when dating are the concepts that some of you ladies really do want, and maybe even really do need to hear about and understand.

So for better or for worse, here goes…

Having evolved over thousands of years from nomadic hunter-gatherer types, men have a certain inherent drive when it comes to seeking out eligible females. Fueled by instinct, raw emotion, and sometimes no small amount of Tequila, men 'hunt' for women in much the same way they searched for food many thousands of years ago.

For instance, we approach the whole dating scene in an extraordinarily logical fashion.

To begin with – we set goals. How can you ladies find the right man if you don't have a specific goal or target in mind? Men, on the other hand, typically set simple goals; we want to meet and have outrageous sex with women. Easy.

No, seriously.

Now we'll try to make this just as easy for you ladies.

First things first: What kind of man are you really looking for? What is your target?

You ladies need to set some simple goals! For example: what kind of man do you want to meet? Big and tall or short and slim? A professional-type guy or the burly workman variety? You will also need to define why it is you want to meet him and where are you most likely to meet that kind of individual. Bear in mind there are no Cadillac's hiding in the bottom of Cracker Jack boxes, and there are no decent and self-respecting men to be found face down on the bar at happy hour!

You have to know what you are shooting for, so you have to know what you want.

If you don't know what kind of man you want...
you will probably never find him.

Relationships and life are exactly the same. If you don't have that target, if you don't have a specific goal in mind, whether it's love, lust, or your perfect partner, you'll never hit it.

The old analogy is so true. If we gave you a bow and arrow, and told you to shoot at the wall – even if you hit the wall, you have no idea exactly how well you've done. But if we draw a target on the wall, a big red circle with smaller circles towards the middle – then we tell you to shoot the arrow. The closer you come to the center, the better, then you'll know exactly what you're aiming for and you know exactly how well you did.

If you just keep shooting your arrows with no targets, you'll never know how well or how poorly you're really doing.

Next, learn to choose your 'hunting grounds' wisely. There is precious little use looking for an art lover and fine food aficionado at a World Wrestling Federation match!

Obviously you have to set some goals. Think back to all your previous lovers and try to determine the kind of man that makes you the happiest. Odds are you will be able to come up with a fairly specific profile that will rule out certain kinds of men.

Most importantly, you'll be able to separate those men who think that 'foreplay' is the warm-up period that takes place before the playing of the national anthem at sporting events!

Ok, so assuming now that you know who you are looking for and where you might find him, how will you know if it's really him once you start the conversations?

You have to know who your audience is.

For example, you don't try to sell a Porsche to a person that has no job, correct?

Some of you may already be doing this, without even knowing you are!

Use all of those "getting to know you" questions.

For example: *What do you do for a living? Where did you grow up?*

This is called **qualifying.**

If you do not know to whom you're talking to, then you are truly wasting your *most* valuable assets – your time and your energy. Don't spend an entire evening speaking to some "smoothie" at the bar who has a wedding ring on. Or, if you are looking for a life partner, don't spend all night talking to a guy in his late forties who professes to be a professional bachelor!

Ask questions and listen to the answers. Watch for the clues that may make him right – or wrong – for you! Chances are, after a couple of drinks he is going to say or do something that will tip you off as to his true colors. Listen for the clues that may make him "unqualified" for you.

Do not ignore the warning signs! If your red lights start to flash it is probably for a reason. If past episodes of substance abuse or domestic violence checker his past it is very likely they will raise their ugly heads again somewhere down the road. If a man does not demonstrate basic courtesy, fails to hold a door open for you, or appears unresponsive to your basic needs – beware! If this is your date on his best behavior, what is it going to be like after 20 years of marriage?

Above all else – learn to handle some rejection. Some guys will measure up, some won't, so what? Next! This is the same advice I've give to men all across the country. Even if you do meet a terrific guy who seems right for you and it just doesn't click – NEXT!

His disinterest in you is not a personal indictment of your personality.

The guy may have another unresolved love interest, or he may have some kind of deep rooted emotional block that prevents him from recognizing the girl of his dreams when he meets her. Whatever the reason…move on!

Develop an instinct for men and the many attributes that combine to make them who and what they are. Above all, be observant!

You can also always tell the women who just get crushed by rejection, because they are the same women who you'll hear say, "I'm not dating anymore. I'm so tired of being hurt."

You've never, at least I've never, heard a guy say, "That's it…that girl didn't want to have sex with me, so I'm just never going to sleep with any other women ever again!"

"Some will, Some won't, So What…. NEXT!"

No matter what, be confident and resilient enough in your own right to understand and accept that just because you might find somebody attractive does not mean that the feeling is immediately reciprocated, if at all. Learning to handle rejection, without going into a major emotional and physiological tailspin, is one of the keys to cultivating a healthy dating lifestyle.

To recap, let us remind you that in order to date like a pro you have to set goals.

First, you can't bag a prince if you are aiming at frogs.

Second, learn to qualify your targets. He may be the nicest most charming guy in the world, but if he is forty-three, addicted to anti-depressants and still living at home with mom – you might want to reconsider.

And finally, do not take it as a personal attack on your Earthly existence, just cause some guy doesn't respond to your advances or chooses not to continue dating you. Boys are like streetcars – just be patient and there will be another one along in a moment!

Q: *So what you're saying is, that the key to handling rejection, is understanding that there are plenty more guys out there for you and just to keep on looking?*

Even if it's not plenty – there's at the very least <u>one</u>. One great one. Your one! Your prince.

Remember that there really is someone out there for everyone. It is still your choice!

Remember, you girls control your own futures, so choose your targets wisely, aim high and good hunting!

-CHAPTER -9-

Acrophobia... "The fear of falling!"

It's the scariest thing… love without a net.

I actually borrowed this title from a song that a friend of mine, Jason Hook, wrote years ago. The song was never released to the public and may never be, but I've always loved it, and I loved the concept.

A lot of women say that they are, "just looking for a good time, nothing too serious and that they just want to have some fun!" Sorry ladies, I don't believe you.

The first chance that you get, you go right for the man's Achilles tendon…commitment.

This is OK, just don't lie to yourselves.

I know the minute you meet a 'nice guy", you're writing your first name with his last name just to see how it looks and how it sounds! Aren't you?

Relax, this is completely natural – but it's also very dangerous from a 'new' relationship standpoint.

This has been a recurring subject in our conversations and interviews with women.

Women ask us all the time,

Q: "Why did he say he was going to call, and then not?"

Q: "Why does he run away whenever we start to talk about love or commitment?"

If you were to poll a panel of men and ask them when and how it was they fell in love with their women you would likely be met with stony silence, a few shrugs, a couple of head shakes and at least one of them would make a run for the door. Why? Because for the most part, men fear falling in love, that's why. Worse still – until we're ready, we hate even talking about the dreaded 'L-word'.

There is a theory between prominent sociologist's and historians that men invented war to circumvent falling in love. The theory is sound and, in fact, most men would rather stick hot needles in their eyes than spend a quiet evening discussing their feelings for a woman – especially if his buddies found out about it later!

The reasons why men fear love and long-term commitment are many and complex. Chances are the man wants, and in fact *needs,* the relationship to work and advance as much as women do. The trouble is men tend to get hung up on the little things like homes, mortgages, kids, college tuition's and all those other 'adult-type' responsibilities that go along with long-term relationships. But we'll come back to this is a moment.

So, back to the question, **"Why did he say he was going to call, and then not?"**

Answer #1. He's a Jerk

There are guys out there, believe it or not, who just collect women's telephone numbers as trophies. It's a, pardon the pun, 'Numbers game'. It's totally an ego trip. Whether they ever call the number or not is inconsequential.

The more numbers, the more the guy feels like a stud. He may just be a player and doesn't really care if he hurts your feelings. Especially if he thinks or knows he can get away with it. If he's the guy that shows up at your door at 3:00 in the morning after not calling you, and after not being nice to you, and you still let him in – then what do you expect?

Some men are just nothing but big – "little boys". And you have to treat them that way. If a child is bad, and you let him continue to be bad, then he's not going to stop on his own. If the guy is a jerk and you let him be a jerk – then he's going to continue to be a jerk!

Answer #2. He may just not like you?

He may just not be interested in you. And remember, that's Ok!

He may be an OK guy and took your number to be polite. Now that he's not under the pressure of being in front of you, maybe he just doesn't want to hurt your feelings. Remember the lesson we learned in Chapter 8 about how to handle rejection.

Some will, Some won't, So What…NEXT!

Just because a man doesn't call you doesn't mean that he's a liar or a jerk.

If you start down that road where every guy that it doesn't work out with is a jerk, you'll start to be "that woman" that we all know who just hates all men, because – they're men.

Men can sense that a mile away, and that woman is not going to be the mother of their children!

OK, this brings us to the title. Acrophobia and "the fear of falling."

Answer #3 He's Terrified!

Pay close attention, because this may get confusing.

Maybe he really does like you! Maybe you've finally found the right guy and believe it or not, he's just a little bit scared. Ladies, I know you'll find this hard to believe, but it is so true. He could just be nervous, especially if there was alcohol involved in the initial getting of your number! The next morning comes, and the alcohol wears off and so does the "liquid" courage! *(See #9 on Why Sleep Alone? VOL. I.)*

Commitment to a long-term relationship is, for most men, akin to the leap from boyhood to manhood.

A long-term relationship to a man is not just 'love' without a net – it's 'life' without a net and that fills most of us with a kind of dread usually reserved for firing squads and tax audits. By committing to a girl – just *one* girl – we are, in our minds at least, admitting that a certain part of our lives is over and that a new and uncharted phase is about to begin. He says good-bye two-seater British sports cars, wind-surfers and all-night bull sessions with the boys and says hello to little league games, dinner parties and endless suburban streets lined with SUV's!

Hence, what you women are up against is something much, much bigger than you know. What you are actually battling is 30 million years of evolution. To actually admit that he has fallen in love with you and commit to a long-term relationship the male must first undergo a significant psychological shift in his thinking and his overall approach to life. For you gals, falling in love may be the logical progression in the maturation process of a relationship. Whereas for us men, until we are ready, it can be like a root canal – only without the freezing!

Even if deep down inside it's what HE REALLY WANTS!

The remedy to all of this is, of course, *patience.* A smart woman must recognize that falling in love for the male involves different thought patterns and is perceived by men as having 'life altering' ramifications. There is typically a certain emotional gyration that the male must undergo before he can fully and completely commit to a relationship. For instance, while taking the "Heather Locklear" posters off the wall and then insisting on matching cutlery might seem like one small step for you; it is likely a giant leap for him.

"IF" you think this guy has a shot at being a keeper, a prince, then the best advice I can give to you ladies is to RELAX. Forever is a *very* long time and if you're looking for this to be the relationship that you've been dreaming of then, …a day, a week, a month – it really doesn't matter in the greater scheme of things.

By the same token, the male must be made to understand that all women seek some kind of direction in a relationship, and are not content to leave things 'open-ended'. Clear and frequent communication is the key. A woman must be clear about her goals and expectations for the relationship, and a man must be allowed some time to adjust to the thought of a life dramatically changed forever.

By exercising some patience and allowing her man to adjust to the idea of falling and being in love, the successful woman can and will find and marry a prince of her very own. She will have the unique privilege of watching her man take the figurative leap from boyhood into manhood.

If he really is your prince…then trust me, he'll be worth the wait!

-CHAPTER 10-
Friends, Lovers and Lonely Saturday Nights

Originally I was going to call this, "Wishful Thinking…What is he really saying?"

As men we have found that, unfortunately, when it comes to affairs of the heart, women sometimes hear but they don't *listen*. In other words, we have observed that in many instances women hear only what they want to hear from a man…and block out the rest. This, I feel, is perhaps one of the prime reasons why women seem to suffer more than men from the consequences of meeting and dating new people.

Not convinced? Well, consider this; you will rarely hear a man say, "Gosh, she's the perfect woman" and then go on to list all of the horrible things that she has done to him. Conversely, how many times have you heard that come from another woman? On countless occasions we have heard women make all the heartbreaking disclaimers,

"But he says he loves me and he's going to leave his wife."

I actually knew a woman who was dating a man; we won't call him a gentleman, who refused to give her his home phone number! Three months into the 'relationship' and all she had was his cell phone number! Please, ladies, for heaven's sake – wake up! If your red lights are flashing – there is a reason! It is not enough to *hear* – you've actually got to *listen*, too!

Odds are a man is telling you the truth and you're just not hearing it, or you are only choosing to hear that which you want to hear. Either way, it's a sure fire way to heartache and no way to find your prince!

It is critically important for your own mental and emotional health to correctly categorize the nature of each relationship.

It is in every woman's best self-interest to invest some honest thought as to 'which way is up' in every relationship she involves herself in. Is so-and-so a friend, or is he a lover? Do I really care for this man and is he right for me, or – am I just passing the time?

It's important for your own mental and emotional health to figure out what each relationship really is. Whatever it is – that's ok, but don't allow yourself to be fooled into believing that maybe there is something more than there really is.

That's very, very dangerous.

I have a dear female friend who always seems so surprised when her on again/off again boyfriend shows up at the door at 3:00 AM on Thursday night. (Coincidentally, his boys' night out!) She is always so happy to see him, they always have great sex, and then she wonders why she can't find him on a Saturday night. Any Saturday night.

By the same token, if you have a male friend who fusses over you, buys you gifts and sits patiently at your feet while you paint your toe nails – it is likely that he is in it for more than just casual companionship. He probably is making his personal investment in you that he wants to pay off. Will it?

This is the reason for this particular title. You have to honestly categorize your relationships. Don't misunderstand me – this is really difficult.

The next question has been asked of me over and over. The following stories are true, only the names have been changed to protect the not-so innocent.

Q: Why is he confusing me?

I'm sorry to say, I'll bet you that he's already told you his real intentions and you've chosen not to listen.

For example, if you live in Florida and his "ex" (with his baby) lives in Texas, and every time she calls him he jumps on a plane to fly to Texas…I'm sorry. He's screaming at you without having to say a word. He has major unfinished business in Texas and you should run, not walk in the opposite direction. Any other direction! He's talking, and once again, if you're still hanging around—you've chosen not to listen.

(This by the way is a true story!)

Love really is a little blind and many women stumble through relationships with their own personal blinders on. Is it love or is it lust? Is he a lover or just a friend? Is he right for me or just for right now? These are all questions you must ask yourself. Be honest and don't dupe yourself into seeing or hearing something that is not there.

> ### The truth is out there –
> ### you've just got to pay attention to it!

Men have very few modes that they operate under:

A) He's either gotten what he wants—game over.

B) He's realized he can't get what he wants—game over.

C) But if there is still something he wants, and he thinks he has a shot at getting it? Game on! Are you really still in his particular game, and more to the point – do you really want to be?

Men will reveal themselves in a thousand little ways. By learning to interpret men correctly a woman can gain the upper hand and correctly identify just what a man's true intentions are. For example, men lie. (No, really, sometimes unfortunately we do!)

Do we have lust in our hearts for you and only for you? Is there a future in 'us'?

Would we forsake a Saturday with the guys to spend all day shopping with you?

Is it possible that these questions could be answered with answers that are less than the truth? Sure.

But by correctly learning to interpret what we men are actually saying, a smart woman can save herself from the heartache caused by the feckless croaking of a thousand toads. She can learn to identify the exact nature of a relationship and then decide for herself if it is something that she wishes to pursue. By listening and not merely hearing what a man says, a woman can deduce for herself what her partner is thinking and get some bearing on what exactly his designs are for the relationship.

Now as a clarification, I know I'm talking a little as if only women are going through their lives with some kind of blinders on. The truth is, it's not just women. It's people.

I believe the old saying, "Love is blind" is true!

And all I'm saying is that I think it's a little deaf too. That's all.

Believe me, men also suffer from this "deafness" caused by love almost as much as you women do. We just don't admit it, because…well, we're men.

As painful as it may be, just learn to put him into the right category, and then if you have to – go do something else, with someone else on that Saturday night.

That's got to be your decision and I know it isn't easy! We men are sometimes complex creatures full of subtle emotions and conflicting desires. Fortunately for you women, a lot of the time we mostly just feel hungry or we just want to have sex – although not necessarily in that order. The challenge for a woman is in determining which way a man's compass-needle is pointing and then determining for herself if she is going to go that way with him…or not!

But if you listen, you'll have a lot less questions without answers.

And as a final note on this particular subject – princes are usually *not* good liars.

- CHAPTER 11-
Don't Ask vs. Don't Tell!

I haven't yet had anyone, anywhere, convince me that it's a good idea to go through your past lovers, relationships, conquests (or whatever you want to call them) with a new lover or new potential mate. It's true, that some things are better left unsaid. As a matter of fact, I considered changing the title of this chapter to, "Some Things Are Better Left Unsaid!"

It all comes down to the concept of 'over-sharing' versus 'under-sharing'.

Once you have found your prince, or are being courted by a likely prospect, you will have to find a healthy balance between saying too much and offering too little. Generally speaking, most men will agree with the concept of 'don't ask and don't tell'.

What is in the past should, by all accounts, remain in the past. Especially if you think your current lover would be overly sensitive to, or hurt by, the information. In our experience, most men really do not want to know too much about a woman's past lovers and, in particular, her past sexual experiences. Chalk it up to the fragile male ego if you will, but – and trust me on this ladies – talking about having done the bump-and-grind with some 22 year old "Adonis" while on your Greek getaway summer vacation will likely do little to cement your current relationship or strengthen the bonds between you and a new potential prince!

Call me crazy, but people simply have a tough time imagining his or her lover with anyone else, let alone somebody younger or possibly more attractive! By the same token, a decent man should take care not to try and impress you with a list of his sexual conquests either. If he is a gentleman, he will not bore you with countless renditions of past love affairs, or just where and how he came to know that 'special' position that you have both come to love so much!

Never lie about your past; rather always be cautious about what information you choose to share.

Now the argument on the other side of the coin is always, "Don't you want to know what kind of a girl she was, or in your case ladies, what kind of guy he was, before he was with you?"

My answer has always been…NO!

I've always maintained that if I like or even love that person today – I know that person is the sum total of all of his or her experiences, **good or bad**. I call all of these experiences their "footprints." I'm not going to judge her on something she did last month, last year or especially 10 years ago. And in reality, it would be unfair of her to judge me either.

We've all done some things in our lives that we may not be too proud of, and it's better to chalk them up to education or life lessons and leave them far behind.

Of course, this policy has its limits. Current lovers have a right to know of any sexually transmitted diseases you might have, or may have became exposed to in the past. Giving your present lover a case of 'the dose' is no way to build a trusting relationship. In today's world, it may even be prudent to 'exchange papers' as it were, so as to prove to the other that there exists no fear of contracting anything unsightly or potentially life threatening!

So the question remains; how far does one go when revealing details about their past – particularly their sexual past – to someone they are serious with? Well, as long as what you choose to withhold does not have the potential to come back around and ultimately hurt your lover, then you are likely in the clear.

Let's face it, we all have skeletons in our closets; but that too is best left in the past! The truth is, when looking back, we have all done things that we regret and even cringe about after the fact. Provided the deed does not have the potential go off like an emotional landmine somewhere down the road, leave it where it belongs – in the drawer marked 'ancient history'.

Both men and women must also take care not to judge a person based on whatever information they choose not to share with us about their past. Most people have had at least one relationship they would rather not talk about.

After all, we are human. Just because we once got drunk and danced naked in a toga doesn't mean we would not make responsible husbands and fathers or wives and mothers in the future. That was a long time ago, back when we were young and foolish, and well… we were young and foolish!

> ### *Like it or not,*
> ### *we are the sum total of all that we have seen*
> ### *and what (or who) we have done.*

When it comes to past history it is important to remember that your current beau is the result of all of the experiences he has had to date, both good and bad. So try not to be a hypocrite – don't ask *and* don't tell. Be selective about the details you choose to share. Too much information has the potential to really hurt someone and drive a wedge into a promising relationship. Too little information and you risk having embarrassing encounters with former lovers. So just be selective about the details that you share. Better to leave some of that in the "don't tell" part of the program. Trust me on this one ladies.

Let some of the more private experiences remain your own little secrets that you can draw on quietly if need be. The experiences are yours and you own them. Don't ever throw them away and don't ever lose them. But chose to share what you are sure won't hurt the other person.

Q: How do you think a woman should handle jealousy, from herself and from a man?

It's the same answer really.

Jealousy, in men and women is created and perpetuated by a lack of self-confidence in the jealous party. Sometimes just by leaving out some of your past, then you can give your current partner fewer reasons to be jealous.

The very human temptation when we're feeling threatened, is to lash out – to hurt. Fight the temptation to tell you partner your past conquests or secrets just to hurt them, or just to make yourself feel more special.

Remember, "There are two ways to create the tallest building in any town. Either build the tallest building…or tear down all the other buildings around it." Always try to work on making yourself feel better, rather than making everyone else around you feel worse.

Ladies, what's past *is* past. You're working on the future! You really don't have to know all his little secrets. Let him keep a few skeletons in his closet and keep a couple in your own. You sure don't want to tell him something about your past that might scare him off.

That would be foolish. Building trust and intimacy in a relationship has a lot to do with when and where to draw the line about your past experiences. When you do find your prince, be careful not to let your previous adventures taint what could prove to be a very promising future. Use your common sense and decide for yourself when not to ask…and when not to tell.

The feelings you save could be your own!

-CHAPTER 12-

Love, Lust and the Search for the Perfect Partner!

> *The perfect partner is someone you can talk to about nothing for extended periods of time... A lifetime.*

There isn't enough room or time on a thousand pages to tell each of you what is 'perfect' for *you*. But there are a few things that I have to go over so that you do find the 'perfect partner' for you.

Sometimes the best way to figure out what you *do* want is to first figure out what you *don't* want. Again, this is why it's so important for you to be honest with yourself when you are dealing with these, the most powerful of emotions.

Love and lust; can you tell the difference? Lust is very good because it is usually the initiator for what will become love. It is said that real love, like an expensive sweater, lasts and lasts, while lust, like a cheap tablecloth – fades very quickly. When navigating your way through the miasma of any relationship it will be important to understand the definition of both love and lust – and how to tell the two apart.

Lust is good. Lust is even great. Men *love* lust. Lust leads to two people doing all sorts of wild and wonderful things. Like long walks in the rain, sex in elevators, love notes slipped under doors, sex in phone booths, flowers delivered to the office, sex in your parents house after everyone has gone to sleep and you've stuffed a pillow behind the headboard so it won't wake up your little brother in the next room. (Who is probably wide-awake and listening through the wall anyway!)

Lust is often referred to in a more clinical environment as the time of 'Eros'. This is defined as the initial stage of the relationship when you simply cannot get enough of each other. You are absolutely consumed with each other and the things and times you share become uniquely your own, full of passion and a burning sense that this person is more than just a part of your life – this person is life itself.

Lust is quite often the measure of a relationship while in the bedroom, while love on the other hand, is what takes place in the rest of the house.

The trouble is, the Eros stage of a relationship usually does not last. While it often burns with the intensity of a thousand suns, its life span is typically finite. It is what lust changes into that is ultimately important for the long-term health of any relationship. If you are lucky, and if you have found the perfect man for you, the molten lava of lust may cool and settle into the glowing embers of 'love'.

So now… the hard part. What do you do between all the lovemaking? This is going to be the true test. This is going to decide everything.

What transpires between lovemaking is the ultimate test of a relationship!

Maybe we need some definitions?

What is love then? Poets have struggled with this particular definition for centuries.

Love is making a note to remember her parent's birthdays, memorizing what she takes in her coffee, rubbing her feet, touching her cheek without reason or sharing a laugh with her that only the two of you understand. Love is saying everything the other person needs to hear to calm them in a crisis – in a single look.

You'll know you have found your prince when even the average things take on another dimension. When food shopping, or lawn raking, or even changing a dirty diaper are all somehow different because *he* is there.

Q: So with that as a definition of love… how do we tell the difference between lust and love?

I'm not really sure that any one person is qualified to answer that question, but I will tell you how I finally figured it out. There was a change in my perspective. All of a sudden

I went from the place in my head where I was saying, "Why should I be with this woman" to – "why shouldn't I?" From there the next leap was, "Why shouldn't I be with her" to –

"I can not imagine myself being without this woman!"

Just like in the movies and in the fairy tales, real love hit me like a ton of bricks. The question was no longer "if"…it was just a question of "when"? I think the real answer to how you tell the difference is honesty. You'll know. Deep inside, the little voices that we all have are usually fairly accurate, and for some reason we usually choose to ignore them. Don't. If it doesn't feel right, then it probably isn't.

I've spoken to a number of women who say that they are 'OK' with being alone.

Some women I know resign themselves to months, or even years without a "significant other" in their lives. Remember the old saying, "Loving can cost a lot, but <u>not</u> loving can cost a whole lot more!"

Life is a journey not a destination. Trips are almost without exception more fun with a partner to share the experiences with than by yourself. All I'm saying is to be honest enough with yourself to determine love vs. lust.

Is this a weekend trip or is it a *life* trip? There is a very big difference, and I think if you're honest with yourself, you'll see the differences clearly.

By learning to spot the differences between love and lust you greatly increase your chances of finding a prince and making a good life for yourself. Too often women confuse the two, only to find years down the road that their significant other is indeed just a frog in princely clothing!

So, if as soon as you are finished making love, he all of a sudden has somewhere to go that he miraculously remembered…watch out! This is a very bad sign. This probably means that this particular relationship has a bad foundation to build on. You can't build a building on sand. You have to build it on bricks to withstand the weight, otherwise it will collapse. Relationships are exactly the same.

If they have a lousy foundation, no matter how erotic or exciting the beginning is, once that inevitably starts to change – you're in for some major problems and probably some heartache. This was just lust with no real love in sight!

With regards to the perfect partner, the only advice that I want to give here is personal. The perfect partner is going to be obviously different for everybody, but in all the personal ads I've read and all the interviews I've been involved in, the women all seem to be saying the same things I was. I was looking for a "partner" in the true sense of the word. I don't believe the old saying that when you get married the two hearts or two entities become one.

That's not true. We're still two people who have entered into a "partnership." Granted, it's hopefully the greatest partnership of your life, but by remembering that it is a partnership you will never stop taking responsibility for your half!

Or, at least your 51%. Some people, and I agree, believe that all partnerships, business and relationships, should actually only ever be

51% VS 49%, just so you never give up your control, or more importantly, your responsibility for yourself.

I'm not talking about financially here; I'm talking about emotionally. If either party stops carrying their weight, then there are going to be some bad feelings and then eventually problems.

All great partnerships: love, friendships or business – all have to have the cornerstone of communication. That's why if he runs away after sex, you know that the communication part of the partnership is weak or maybe even non-existent.

Again, this is an early warning sign of future problems. Try to imagine a large company where the two managing partners can't even communicate. More than likely, they're going to go "out of business," and unfortunately…so are you.

Q: So are you saying that the "Perfect Partner" is just someone that you can talk to?

No – they have to have it all. And you'll know. Lust then love, friendship and understanding.

Great partners are obvious. Not just to themselves, but to those around them.

His strengths help her weaknesses and her strengths help his weaknesses. That's the perfect partner.

A perfect partner is the person who always makes you feel the best about 'you'.

That's no frog…that's your prince.

-CHAPTER -13-
Women's Top Ten Questions!

Here's what we did.

We sent out Emails and conducted telephone interviews all over the world asking…

"If you could give a man, any man, truth serum…what would be the top three questions that you would ask him, to have answered honestly!"
The response was amazing!
(And thank you to everyone that spoke to us or E-mailed us.)

This ladies, really is *the* guide to **Reading His Mind!** (www.readinghismind.com)

It didn't matter if they were single or married, happy or not so happy. We quickly realized that there were going to be as many different questions as there were people asking them. But just as we had hoped and expected, there was enough overlap to start to compile the Top Ten List for you!

So here it is. These were the most frequently asked questions…by *you.*

NOTE: Once again, the following is a frank question and answer session. We offer this to you, the female reader, in an effort to further clarify the difference in the way men think compared to women. We compiled these questions and attempted to provide 'typical' male answers hoping that the information contained herein will assist you in achieving your goal of reading his mind and finding your prince.

Question #1: Why do men cheat?

No, the answer here is not going to be, "Because all men are pond scum!" Sorry.

There are actually a number of reasons why men cheat.

Number one is really no more than pure selfishness. Remember what we spoke about regarding motivators? There are really only two: (I) fear of pain, and (II) desire for pleasure. Because a man is selfish, his own desire for pleasure becomes more important than his own fear of pain – or even his partner's pain. A man might simply care more for his own feelings than his partner's feelings. Cruel, we agree, but true nonetheless.

Next, a man might cheat because he feels unfulfilled in the relationship, either emotionally or sexually. There are a thousand reasons why a relationship could be deemed as 'unfulfilling'. However, whatever the symptoms, the end result will always be the same – people will look to be fulfilled somewhere else. It's only human nature.

Also, there is likely a lack of basic respect within the relationship. If a man cheats he is either lacking ethically and morally, or, there was no groundwork laid for respect in the relationship from the very beginning. If a man has no respect for himself or his partner (or for some reason she either lacks or fails to demand any respect for herself) then, once again, human nature will take it's course and the man will stray.

Lastly, and this is a subject open to quite a bit of conjecture, *men fear aging*. For the male, 'pulling the trigger' can be likened to proving, if to no one other than himself, that he still has what it takes to bed one or more beautiful women. It's all got to do with 'spreading our plumage' and still believing that we are the "man" – so to speak! Men like to feel as though they can still hunt like a young lion if, and when, they choose to.

If a man is truly maturing in the relationship he will soon come to realize that the short-term gains – though enticing – are simply not worth the long-term losses. Though we are not above doing a little window-shopping, we know in the end that our girl is the best. Like the man said, "Why go out for hamburger when you have steak right here at home?"

Question #2: Why do men always want what they can't have?

I believe that this particular emotion is completely natural. It's how you act on it that can become a specific problem.

It all has something to do with the fable about the little doggy with the bone in his mouth that looks at his reflection in the water. He sees another little doggy with an even bigger bone, and he drops the bone he's got to go after the illusion of something better.

I think the women who had asked this particular question were dealing with some personal insecurity issues, possibly because the person that they were referring to had a wandering eye.

So my answer is… Why do people want what they can't have?

It's human nature and not always bad. Handled correctly, this is the trait that will inspire people to great things, just to achieve or receive something that they don't have…yet.

It's when it's handled incorrectly that it gets out of control for men and women, not just men.

Question #3: What happened to romance? Why don't men buy flowers anymore?

This question shocked me! We do! I have a friend who hired an airplane to drag one of those "happy birthday" signs for his wife – right past their house! I have another friend who filled his girlfriends office up with a truckload of flowers, just to make a first impression. What an impression! (They are now married.)

I still buy flowers all the time! I write love-notes and even write and record love songs! And I don't think we're the only ones. Romance is not dead, but it is a two way street. When was the last time you ladies wrote a little love note to us? Yes, it is just as important to us.

I promise. My best answer would be that romance is not dead, and women should learn to lead by example. If you want your men to be romantic – then be romantic too! It may not be the answer you wanted, but if you lead, I promise – he will follow.

Question #4: Why is it men have more fun with their friends than with their partner or their spouse?

I think the best answer here is, we don't have more fun – it's a different kind of fun.

And that's ok. You shouldn't be threatened by the fun that he has with his friends. He should also never be threatened by the different kind of fun and conversations that I'm sure you have with your friends either.

Never put the pressure on yourself to be all things to your mate. It's unrealistic and will only cause you pain. When he wants to do the male "thing"...let him.

When you feel like you need a woman's perspective on something – seek it out.

These things are natural.

Try to be not so sensitive and enjoy the fact that your man is happy. Hopefully, he's enough of a gentleman to return the thought and let you have your fun with your friends too. The key here is moderation. Just as long as he's not with 'the boys' six nights a week!

That's not fair and could be a sign of a larger, more serious problem. Be careful.

Question #5: What do men really think about going 'Dutch' or even letting a woman pay for them? Does it make them feel insecure?

In a healthy relationship, either partner should feel comfortable picking up the tab!

Some guys would be really uncomfortable with this and here's the reason why. Ego.

The male ego is a very funny and fragile thing.

A healthy relationship is a partnership, so there should be some of this, but that darn ego- thing just gets in the way. If the guy is a gentleman, he's going to be fighting thousands of years of history, where the "man" is supposed to take care of the woman.

As a man, there are just some things that we feel that we should take care of. I mean no disrespect here, quite the opposite. I like to open car doors, and I still like to take care of my woman. Physically, spiritually and financially. It makes me feel good. I try to let myself be taken care of sometimes too because I know it means a lot to her to take care of me. But I admit that sometimes it's difficult.

CAUTION: The trouble, however, starts when one of the two *expects* the other to pay. This can lead to all kinds of heartburn and bad feelings.

Question #6: What do men consider "high maintenance" in a woman?

Originally, I was going to say, "the same thing that a woman considers high maintenance in a man." But as I thought about it, that's not really true. On closer inspection, I feel that women who are deemed 'high-maintenance' are really women who take an emotional toll on a man. Let me explain...

Men don't want to "work" at a relationship. Women don't mind work, but they want results. So my best answer would be that a man considers a woman who is a lot of "work" – high maintenance. So now, what's work?

Well, to a man – work is anything that doesn't go smoothly. He just wants for it all to go smoothly. Men, in general, hate confrontation with their partners. If they wanted a fight, they would just go back to whatever their job is and fight with whomever today's villain is in today's particular rat race!

We fight the traffic, we fight for a good living, and we even fight for a good parking spot! We're idiots really. But we do know what we want. And we do know what we don't want. We want to find shelter in our relationships, not just more grief of a different color.

Here's some advanced mathematics for you. (No, you don't need a calculator for this.)

I have personally witnessed this a thousand times and I can tell you the results are irrefutable.

First, we need to review the age-old scale of external beauty that ranges: 1 through 10.

The number 1 being less than particularly pleasing to the eye, and the number 10 being a 'perfect' score. Next, you must understand that we men also have a second, very private, hidden scale.

We have the quiet, unspoken, secret scale that *is* the true test. This is the scale that you ladies are trying to rate well on, whether you ever really know it or not.

This is called the "Keeper Scale."

Truthfully, this is a much harsher rating system, and the one that is ultimately more important for you to score really high marks on!

Here's how it works.

Let's say that you are a strong number 9 on the external beauty scale but your personality is that of a wildly, out of control, miserable witch! (Sometimes spelled with a B)

Guess what? You fall instantly to a number 3, (if you're lucky) on the keeper scale because your personality has offset your physical beauty.

This is also sometimes referred to as the "Broken Racing Car Syndrome."

All over the World there are women that rank extraordinarily high on the external beauty scale. The problem sometimes lies in what's 'under the hood.'

To continue the analogy, the paint is perfect, the wheels are all chromed and shinny but, time and time again…the darn things motor is broken! What is the sense of a beautiful racing car with no motor?

It may be fun to sit in for a little while, even let your friends see you in it once or twice, but in the long run...where are you going to go? Nowhere.

As you can well imagine, this particular model rates poorly on the 'keeper scale.'

Now conversely, let's say you rank as a strong number 7 on the external beauty scale.

You also possess all of the things that men are looking for in a woman's personality. You're fun, intelligent but not combative, and you just make it easy for us to like you and hang out.

Translated: you make us feel good about...us.

Guess what again? You fly to a strong number 9 or maybe even a number 10 on the keeper scale. You're far ahead of even your prettiest of friends because you understand the secrets of the keeper scale! This is the scale for today's woman who aspires to be more than a broken racing car or some guy's one-night-stand.

My advice to all single women is just *try* to make it easy on him. That isn't easy – but try. He'll love you forever. Be his shelter, not his rain. It may sound corny, but nobody likes the rain.

Women who are deemed 'high-maintenance' are really women who take an 'emotional toll' on a man.

Question # 7: Is it true that men want a "lady" in public and a "prostitute" in the bedroom?

That was really an awkward question, but we are here for honest answers.

So, the answer is…YES.

Next question please.

Question #8: Is it true that men give love for sex and women give sex for love?

No, that is not true. Love has nothing to do with *sex* for a man. If he's going to have sex, he's going to have sex. He wants to have sex with the woman he loves *because* he loves her, but he also just wants to have sex. He's a man. A normal, healthy man likes sex.

On the other hand, women who give sex for love will only ever get temporary love, or even worse they'll get no love back – just sex. I understand that the idea here is really, "Will men fake love to get sex?" The real answer is no, not a gentleman. If he wants to have sex he shouldn't try to call it anything else. If she wants to be in love, she should not confuse love with sex or she will ultimately be disappointed.

Question #9:

We were amazed at how many variations of these next questions that we received.

It seems like women obviously have real questions about direction and about the future. Sometimes, the very distant future. Questions like:

What do you do for a living?

What are your goals?

What do you see yourself doing when you retire?

What is it you want from your life?

What do you want most in a close, intimate relationship?

Those questions were almost as frequent as the most obvious questions a woman wants answered. The questions about 'her'.

What do you look for in a woman?

What qualities in a woman are important to you?

What do guys think about when they think about the "perfect woman?"

What were some of the things you liked best about some of the women you've been closest to?

(Note: Remember this one! It's a great qualifying question.)

What bothers you about dealing with women?

What are men looking for most in women?

And some the most personal and the most basic.

Do you love me?

What do you like most about me?

What made me really happy and amazed me about all these questions was that women out there were doing exactly what we told you to do in Chapter 8.

Qualify, qualify, and qualify again.

All of these are great questions to ask, but not great questions for me to answer.

Great questions for you to ask your man or your "potential partner." Your prince!

The first group of questions, referring to the future, will tell you important facts about what he thinks about himself, and the second group will let you know a little about what he's thinking about you.

They're perfect. Just make sure you're really listening when he answers them!

Here's the one I loved, only because when I read this one I couldn't stop laughing.

I *had* to share the laugh with you ladies.

One of you sent us the Question #10.

Question #10: What made you men ever think that that shirt actually looks good?

Hilarious. Thank you for the chuckle.

And while we're having a little laugh about some of the letters that were received, here are a couple of bonus questions!

Q: Why don't men just admit how much influence their mothers have on their lives?

Oh, we do…("Hi, mom!")

Our mothers have and do continue to influence us our whole life long. After all, this is the woman we first had a relationship with and the one woman who still thinks we are absolutely adorable even when we fail.

Here's an observation for you while we are on the topic of parents. As another one of our famous rules of thumb, we have observed that men tend to marry women similar to their mothers – even in those instances when they claim they are not really all that taken with or close to their mothers. Whereas women, for their part, will generally have only as good a relationship with their man as they do (or did) with their fathers.

I realize these are broad generalizations, however, in my experience they have been closer to the truth then maybe any of us really want to believe. Food for thought.

Q: *So what if they've exchanged #'s and he hasn't called?*

Q: *Should the woman call him?*

Great question and the same answer, over and over again!

"Everything to gain and nothing to lose!" Make the call!

If a frog answers…hang up.

-Chapter 14-
<u>The Wrap Up and What's Next?</u>

We've covered a lot of ground, so let's do a little recap.

So far we've learned that we have…

"Everything to gain and nothing to lose!"

Not just in relationships ladies, but also in life!

Do you want to learn a new language? Go!

Do you want to write a book? Do it! Write it!

You really do have everything to gain and nothing to lose at all. Make this your credo and you'll be amazed how liberating it is. You'll talk to more people, you'll do more – you'll live more. I promise. And that's why you're here, to learn the secrets to happiness. In the end, no one will care if you fail at anything, but the successes will change your life!

Oh yeah, go and talk to that cute guy you've always wanted to talk to.

What exactly do you have to lose?

We learned about …

Love Potions and Flirting: How to make any man fall in love with you.

Remember that men are easy! Just don't sleep with him on the first date! Smiles, eye contact, buy him a drink, ask for his telephone number, but most importantly just be open to the moment and have fun. Be nice. That's all it really takes to make a man fall in love with you. He doesn't want to work that hard, he wants to have fun!

It's been said that, "Most relationships are decided in the first thirty seconds!"

So, do what women do so naturally. Make the man want you! Almost any woman can have any guy she wants by demonstrating even a mild interest in those things that are dear to him.

They all want at least a bit of a chase…so give it to them. Just let him think that it was his idea!

We learned to forgive and forget the 'Sins' of another man.

> *Treat every man that you meet as though he was the first man that you ever met.*
> *For all you know, he could be 'the one' that you end-up spending the rest of your life with!*

Let each new relationship be just that – new. You'll have a much better chance of it working if you allow it to start with a clean slate. If you've had a string of jerks, even divorces for some of you, this is going to be extremely tough, but an absolute necessity.

Let it go. Hopefully he's not like the others, and you're off to a fresh, new and happier time.

R.E.S.P.E.C.T Yourself! You deserve the best!

If you have no respect for yourself…then why should anyone else have any respect for you?

I believe this to be the cornerstone of a healthy mind and a healthy relationship. You're not broken inside; there is nothing wrong with you! Understand that you as a person deserve a good life and it will begin to unfold right in front of your eyes. No magic, just life.

> *We take out of life what we believe we deserve.*

If you believe that you are worth $5.00 per hour, you'll earn it. If you really believe that you are worth $50.00 per hour, then you'll earn that too. It's all up to you. This is not easy, but you have to do it for yourself everyday. If deep down inside you believe that you deserve to be fat—then you will never be thin.

You control your thoughts, and your thoughts control your emotions. You control your emotions.

There is nothing that you've done in this life that you are being punished for.

And that's all you're doing, punishing yourself.

In order to become healthy you must believe that you deserve to be healthy.

You've heard, "A journey of a thousand mile's begins with one step."

Take the step in your own mind first. There is no other place to start.

The Bargain Bin: You *will* get what you pay for.

He's probably really good looking...

He's probably really popular...

You're probably the envy of all your girlfriends...and you're probably still miserable.

Why do we love those people that are so bad for us? Stop trying to save him and save yourself! You don't need to save anybody just to make yourself feel better. It's only ever a quick fix and you ultimately will end up back where you started, with you.

Concentrate on fixing you. It's a much better investment.

Why Kiss A Frog? Your Prince is out there!

Just keep on looking, he is out there.

No, not all men are scum. You just haven't met your "Prince" yet. The key here is not perfect, but perfect for you. Remember, this is a great big world ladies. Six billion people and half of them are men. Be picky. Don't settle. Go ahead, make a "wish list" and stick to it.

It will help you to decide who's the "stud" and who's the "dud." Whatever you do, just make sure that he is a gentleman. All of you deserve at least that! Stay away from manipulators! These kinds of men (and women) usually cause nothing but heartache.

That's no prince…that's a frog!

The Hunting Trip: Learn how to date like a man.

Now you know some of our secrets:

1. Pick your target so you know what you're shooting at.
2. Qualify so you know if what you have in front of you is really what you want.
3. Handle the rejection if it doesn't work out.

"Some will, Some won't, So What…. NEXT!"

Be careful, because if you've really been paying attention, you may end up with more dates than you know what to do with. Remember to listen.

> **"God gave you two ears and only one mouth so you could listen _twice_ as much as you speak!"**

A lot of people want to make it more difficult than it is, but it's not. Pick a target, qualify, listen and ask him for what you want. You might be pleasantly surprised to find out that that's what he wants too! Never quit trying if you really want to be a winner!

Next was,

Acrophobia: The fear of falling!

Through it all, try to maintain a sense of both balance and realism. Men tend to deal in the 'here and now' whereas women, heaven help you, have a very real tendency to think and dream in terms of the 'what if' or 'should be'. Living and making a life with your prince is likely going to be a little different than what you imagined it to be. Be patient.

Q: So, Why doesn't he call you after taking your number?

Q: Why does he run when you talk about commitment?

He's either just a jerk, or he's more afraid then he's ever going to let you know. Not just of you, not just of love and relationships, but of "life" and all the responsibilities that come along with it. Making that jump from "boyhood to manhood" is one of the hardest things he'll ever do.

He's no longer free to be responsible only for himself. Now he gives up being "Peter Pan" and actually has to grow up. Be patient. Once again, if he is the right guy he'll be worth the wait.

Remember that, "Forever is a very long time." If you really are meant to grow old together, be careful not to push him away by trying to force it to happen today! If it's meant to be…it will happen.

If he really is your prince, he will catch you when you fall.

Ok, on to…

Friends, Lovers And Lonely Saturday Nights: Why is he confusing you?

Hearing without listening, or only hearing what you really want to hear causes all the confusion! It's so important for your own mental and emotional help to figure out what "each" relationship is.

If he is just a friend? OK, everybody needs really good friends.

If he's a lover, then that's OK too! Everybody sure needs that as well.

Is he something more? Well, maybe only time will tell.

Be honest with yourself! That's the key to not having lonely Saturday nights. Chances are he's telling you that you're not going to get Saturday nights, and you've chosen not to hear him.

That's not his fault, it's yours.

Love, lust, friend, lover or even maybe something more? Listen. Honestly listen.

And if it's not what you really want or really deserve…NEXT! There is no reason to wait for him on a Saturday night if that's not what you want to do.

Next was,

Don't Ask vs. Don't Tell: The age-old question.

If you really love that person today, then understand that whatever "footprints" he or she has are theirs. Whatever experiences they may have had, good or bad, created that person in front of you today. Don't judge. You cannot change what has happened in the past. Let it go. In reality, it's none of your business what they did when they were younger and more foolish, as we all once were, and they deserve to keep those memories their own.

Remember always that this is a two way street. If you don't really want to tell – then just don't ask. In reality, knowing can only serve to cause pain or even worse, jealousy. Not exactly the great foundation for a healthy relationship that we're all looking for. Leave the past in the past. Forever starts today and goes forward, not backwards. Try to find the healthy balance between over-sharing and under-sharing.

Remember, if God had wanted us to live in the past, he would've installed mirrors on the sides of our heads so we could see where we've been. He didn't.

In Chapter 12 we discussed…

Love, Lust and the Search for the Perfect Partner:

Lust is good. Lust can even be great, but when it turns into love…it's the best.

Eros is going to fade a little bit ladies. It's natural. Don't panic. It's even going to fade more for some than others. That's OK too. Life is a journey, not a destination, and the journey is going to have many different forms and many different landscapes. Try to learn to enjoy each landscape for what it is.

Remember that great partners are obvious to us and to those around us. Great partnerships are usually not a lot of work. They are some work, without question, but not torture.

Lust, then love, friendship and understanding. Using communication and strengths for each other's weaknesses. That's what makes a great partnership.

> **A great partner will never**
> **demand that you lose yourself to them.**

Remember...51% VS 49%...

Always hold on to your 51%! You deserve it!

And remember...nobody is perfect, just perfect for you!

When we rub your feet after a long day without you having to ask, or caress your cheek with the back of our hands for no apparent reason – that's love! The perfect partner is someone you can talk to about nothing for extended periods of time...a lifetime!

In Chapter 13...

Women's Top Ten Questions:

What the heck are men really thinking? Honest answers to all those wonderful questions. Thank you again to all the women who took the time to speak to us or write to us. Without you, there would've been nothing to talk about.

And now we're here at Chapter 14.

What's next?

That's a great question...what is next? The great news ladies is that today is a brand new day. It doesn't matter whether you have been lucky at love or a total disaster so far! With all this new ammunition and information I believe the next phase of your social life should be a whole lot easier and a whole lot more fun.

WHY KISS A FROG? is really all about READING HIS MIND!

At least now you'll understand a little better why he does some of the crazy things he does.

There is hope ladies. Never give up. Never. Your prince is out there. Now go and find him!

Thank you so much Ladies, and Good luck!

-Bonus Chapter -15-
<u>Knowledge is Power!</u>

A **FINAL WORD**:

I just want to leave you with one extra thought. Something special from me… to you.

You've heard it a thousand times in your life that knowledge is power. I'm going to shock you and tell you exactly what you didn't think I was going to say.

That statement is not true. Well, not entirely.

It's not the knowledge that is power. There are brilliant people everywhere who are never really successful at anything, because they never actually do anything with their brilliance.

It's what you do with that knowledge that makes you powerful!

From "**Everything to gain** to **R.E.S.P.E.C.T**"

From "**Why Kiss A Frog**? to **Acrophobia.**"

This is information that really can change your life. But only if you let it!

The secrets that you've just acquired are not really secrets.

> ### *It's been said many times before that*
> ### *there is no new information…*
> ### *there are only new teachers, and new students.*

Much of this you probably already knew down deep inside. You just have to put these ideas into everyday life. You have to put the "train in motion" or it's never going to go anywhere, never going to change anything.

Always remember that you never get a second chance at life. This is it! This is not just a dress rehearsal.

As long as you are here you have to act as if you're not going to get a second chance.

Truth is you probably aren't, so make this one count. What do you have to lose?

If you want something that you've never had before, be willing to do something that you've never done before.

For some of you, that's simply going to be "taking action", for others it's only going to be a matter of refining the ineffective actions you've already been taking.

Life is not a spectator sport. You have to play to win.

Remember that you deserve it. Just keep saying that to yourself, over and over again.

(You really do, you know?)

He's out there somewhere. Your "Prince!"

He's waiting for you. Don't let him down. More to the point, don't let US down.

And most importantly… don't let yourself down.

Because in the end, all this is really about …is you.

Now you have the knowledge. It's up to you to turn it into power!

Just have a great time.

Goodnight ladies and once again, good luck.

Thank you for all of the conversations, and as I always say, **"thanks for listening."**

About the Author

Originally from Toronto Canada, Michael McGahey's world is music, art, laughter, love, friendship and a lifetime of accomplishments.

His artistic career has awarded him scholarships to Art College, song-writing grants by the Canadian Government, hundreds of live performances and having his music released in countries as far away as Japan and Germany.

His business/management/leadership accomplishments pinnacled with the winning of the prestigious 'Man For All Seasons Award' 2001, GLM Group of Companies, Inc.

2002 brought Michael's first successful move into the authoring of Self-Help books, co-writing

WHY SLEEP ALONE? 'An audio Self-Help book for Men', with partner Mitchell Newman.

Finally in 2002, **WHY KISS A FROG**? Your Prince IS Out There!

"Men's Honest Answers to All Women's Questions…About Men! A testament to the fact that successful relationships have more to do with learned behavior, than happenstance or 'lightning striking'."

Michael McGahey is currently living, loving, working and writing in Miami, South Florida.

Special Thanks:

These are the people who make the impossible…possible.

To all the wives, girlfriends, lovers and intimate strangers that I love, have loved, or have loved and lost along the way. Thank you for the inspiration, information and education that I now share. You will never be forgotten.

To My Heroes, Teachers, Partners and Friends:

There has never been a single moment in my life that one of you wasn't there for me.

Whenever I've needed: a friend, a lover or a perfect partner, one of you rescued me.

G. Marshall

(The Brother I've always had, and always wanted. My Hero and Greatest Teacher.)

J. Gleneicki, J. Grinstead, R. Santers

(You are my inspirations in art, music and life!)

To my family: Laura, Barbie, Mirtha and Big Ed.

(I hope Mom is watching and proud.)

To the people who made me sound smart(er?)

S.K. Ross, M. Burns, M. Early, M. Newman.

To my Partner: Mitchell Newman

(You've never let me down, not once, not ever. That's rare.)

To my Friend: Mitchell Newman

(The Brother that I never had, and always wanted. Thank you!)

And To the Love of My Life: Michelle

(You are my breath. Forever, Whatever That Means!)

ALSO BY THE AUTHOR

WHY SLEEP ALONE?

WHY SLEEP ALONE?

WHY SLEEP ALONE? VOL. I. The Men's Edition!

A Self-Help Guide for Men in Printed format. McGahey/ Newman

The complete "How-to-meet" and "How-to-treat Women"

Book – for Men!

"Turns Everyman Into A Ladies Man!"

Available at www.whysleepalone.com

WHY SLEEP ALONE?

WHY SLEEP ALONE? VOL. I. The Men's Edition!

A Self-Help Guide for Men on Audio CD format.

McGahey/ Newman

The complete Audio "How-to-meet" and "How-to-treat Women"

Book – for Men!

"The CD That Turns Everyman Into A Ladies Man!"

Available at www.whysleepalone.com

WHY KISS A FROG? Your Prince <u>Is</u> Out There!

© 2002 BBE, Inc.

WHY SLEEP ALONE? VOL. II. The Women's Edition!

© 2002. All Rights Reserved.

A Self-Help Guide for Women on Audio CD format.

Available at www.whykissafrog.com

Every Woman's Complete Self-Help Guide to Friends, Lovers and

The Search for Her Perfect Partner!

© 2002 BBE, Inc. ANY Unauthorized duplication is a violation of

applicable laws.

Copyrights © 2002, Michael McGahey

Printed in USA. WARNING: All Rights Reserved. Unauthorized

Duplication is a Violation of Applicable Laws.

www.ingramcontent.com/pod-product-compliance
Lightning Source LLC
Chambersburg PA
CBHW051444280526
45785CB00003B/1419